HAL•LEONARD

INSTRUMENTAL PLAY-ALONG

AUDIO
ACCESS
INCLUDED

PLAYBACK+
Speed • Pitch • Balance • Loop

SUPERHERO THEMES

Audio arrangements by Peter Deneff

To access audio, visit:
www.halleonard.com/mylibrary

Enter Code
6428-3898-6250-6612

ISBN 978-1-70513-158-9

For all works contained herein:
Unauthorized copying, arranging, adapting, recording, internet posting, public performance,
or other distribution of the music in this publication is an infringement of copyright.
Infringers are liable under the law.

Visit Hal Leonard Online at
www.halleonard.com

Contact us:
Hal Leonard
7777 West Bluemound Road
Milwaukee, WI 53213
Email: info@halleonard.com

In Europe, contact:
Hal Leonard Europe Limited
42 Wigmore Street
Marylebone, London, W1U 2RN
Email: info@halleonardeurope.com

In Australia, contact:
Hal Leonard Australia Pty. Ltd.
4 Lentara Court
Cheltenham, Victoria, 3192 Australia
Email: info@halleonard.com.au

THEME FROM ANT-MAN
from MARVEL'S ANT-MAN

Flute

Music by CHRISTOPHE BECK

WAKANDA
from BLACK PANTHER

Music by LUDWIG GÖRANSSON

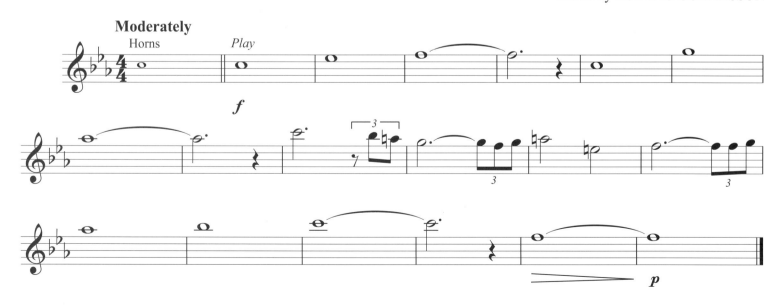

THE AVENGERS

from THE AVENGERS

FLUTE

Composed by
ALAN SILVESTRI

BATMAN THEME

FLUTE

Words and Music by
NEAL HEFTI

CAPTAIN AMERICA MARCH

from CAPTAIN AMERICA

FLUTE

By ALAN SILVESTRI

ELASTIGIRL IS BACK

from INCREDIBLES 2

FLUTE

Composed by
MICHAEL GIACCHINO

IMMORTALS
from BIG HERO 6

Flute

Words and Music by ANDREW HURLEY,
JOE TROHMAN, PATRICK STUMP
and PETE WENTZ

GUARDIANS INFERNO

from GUARDIANS OF THE GALAXY VOL. 2

FLUTE

Words and Music by JAMES GUNN
and TYLER BATES

THE INCREDITS
from THE INCREDIBLES

FLUTE

Music by MICHAEL GIACCHINO

POW! POW! POW! - MR. INCREDIBLES THEME

from INCREDIBLES 2

Flute

Music and Lyrics by
MICHAEL GIACCHINO

IRON MAN
from IRON MAN

FLUTE

By RAMIN DJAWADI

ROCKETEER END TITLES

from THE ROCKETEER

Flute

By JAMES HORNER

THEME FROM SPIDER MAN

FLUTE

Written by BOB HARRIS
and PAUL FRANCIS WEBSTER

X-MEN: APOCALYPSE - END TITLES

from X-MEN: APOCALYPSE

Flute

By JOHN OTTMAN